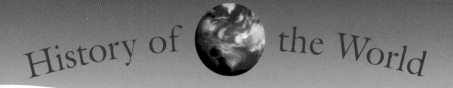

History of the World

Westward Expansion

Cathryn J. Long

KIDHAVEN
PRESS™

THOMSON

─────✦─────™

GALE

San Diego • Detroit • New York • San Francisco • Cleveland
New Haven, Conn. • Waterville, Maine • London • Munich

LIBRARY OF CONGRESS CATALOGING-IN-PUBLICATION DATA

Long, Cathryn J.
    Westward expansion / by Cathryn J. Long.
       p. cm.—(History of the world series)
Includes bibliographical references (p.) and index.
Summary: Explores the time in United States history when western territory was being explored, settled, and turned into states, including the impact this expansion had on native peoples.
    ISBN 0-7377-1383-6 (hardback : alk. paper)
1. West (U.S.)—History—Juvenile literature. 2. West (U.S.)—Discovery and exploration—Juvenile literature. 3. Frontier and pioneer life—West (U.S.)—Juvenile literature. 4. United States—Territorial expansion—Juvenile literature. [1. West (U.S.)—Discovery and exploration. 2. Frontier and pioneer life—West (U.S.). 3. United States—Territorial expansion.] I. Title. II. Series.
    F591 .L63 2003
    978—dc21

                             2002007890

Contents

Chapter One

A Changing Frontier

The United States began its life as a nation in 1776 with the Declaration of Independence. On maps of North America at that time, the United States looks like a thin strip along the shore of the Atlantic. The Appalachian Mountains formed a natural border along most of its western side. The rest of the continent was claimed by Spain, France, and Britain. It was also home to many Native American tribes.

The thin strip would soon grow wider, however. Citizens of the United States were eager to move westward. So, what Americans defined as the "West" was a constantly changing place. At different times in American history, it meant the valley of the Ohio River, the Rocky Mountains, or the Pacific coast. Wherever the West was, most Americans saw it as a land of great promise. The West was full of resources, such as gold, furs of animals, and rich farmland. Anyone, it was said, could make a fortune and a new life out West. And as

Americans moved west, the country grew. Its boundaries would eventually reach from the Atlantic Ocean to the Pacific Ocean and from Canada to Mexico.

This westward expansion was not easy, however. Pioneers faced physical dangers: hot deserts, frozen plains, and wild animals. Worse than these were the dangers from people who wanted the land someone else had claimed. Certainly the native people of North America had the worst experience during the growth of

Covered wagons make their way along the Rocky Mountains.

the United States. For them, the West was nobody's land of promise. It was their own threatened homeland.

As people settled the West, the government of the United States laid claim to each region of wilderness and Indian country. These areas finally became states. This process developed on the first frontier of the new nation: the West that lay just across the Appalachian Mountains.

The Fur Trade

Even before the American colonies became the United States, the fur trade brought Native Americans and Europeans together at the western boundaries of settlement. Indians living along the coast were used to trading furs among themselves, so it was logical to exchange these goods for European beads and tools, blankets, and guns. The Europeans were especially eager to get the water-repellent underfur of the beaver. In Europe this fur was boiled and packed into sheets to make felt, and the felt was used to make hats.

The fur trade encouraged exploration. French and British fur companies sent traders out by canoe or horseback to find Indians willing to sell pelts. Some European Americans trapped animals themselves. These men learned their trade from Indians. Many of them depended on their Indian wives, who knew how to handle furs and how to strike bargains. With Indian help, these fur traders and trappers created many of the first American maps. Several towns . . . such as Detroit . . . began as trading posts for fur.

Fur traders offer Indians supplies for pelts.

Indians were eager to trade for European goods, but the trade also led to fighting. For example, "beaver wars" broke out when the Iroquois began to take over beaver-rich land from other tribes south of the Great Lakes, around 1650. Tribes such as the Huron, who traded with the French, became bitter enemies of the Iroquois, who traded with the British. When France went to war with Britain in the mid-1700s, in the Seven Years' War, Indian tribes fought alongside these nations.

Kentucky, the Second Paradise

The British won the Seven Years' War against France in 1763. As a result, France no longer had a claim to the land between the Appalachian Mountains and the Mississippi River. The peace encouraged colonists to come westward—even though the British tried to make settlement west of the Appalachians illegal.

Daniel Boone was one of the first frontiersmen to fall in love with the land across the mountains from his

Frontiersman Daniel Boone led the first settlers to Kentucky and founded the town of Boonesborough in that region.

Virginia home. Exploring among its woods and beautiful bluegrass meadows, he called this Kentucky region "a second paradise."[1] He and others ignored the fact that several Indian tribes claimed Kentucky as their common hunting ground.

Boone and thirty axmen cleared a broad track, the Wilderness Road, across the Appalachian Mountains. The road allowed settlers' wagons to cross the mountains and reach the **station** of Boonesborough. A station was made up of several log houses around an open area, surrounded by a strong wooden fence called a stockade. Families worked fields outside the stockade, but they could run inside the station for protection when Indian raids threatened. The station pattern of settlement became common all over Kentucky and the Ohio country to the north.

When the new United States defeated Britain in the Revolutionary War, settlement across the mountains became legal, and many more people poured into Kentucky. In 1792 Kentucky became the fifteenth state. It was the first state west of the Appalachians. Kentucky was allowed to join the union with the same rights as all the other states. That set an important example for the future.

New homesteads sprung up all over Kentucky at the end of the Revolutionary War.

The Northwest Territory

Just as Kentucky was filling with settlers after the Revolution, so was the country between the Great Lakes and the Ohio River. This vast area was called the Northwest Territory. In the 1780s Congress passed two laws making rules for the territory.

Congress first declared that the laws of the United States would rule there, not any of the settlements or any tribes. Congress also ordered a way of measuring and selling land. The territory was divided into large districts. The districts were divided into smaller squares, to be sold to settlers. A district could become a state as soon as sixty thousand free men settled there and voted for statehood. Other rules gave settlers certain legal rights. Slavery was outlawed, everyone was to have free travel on the waterways, and the law supported public schools.

However, Indians of the Northwest Territory did not welcome more settlers, whatever their laws. Miami, Shawnee, and other tribes attacked the newcomers. President George Washington sent troops to fight the Indians. Under Miami chief Little Turtle, combined Indian forces won two large battles with the soldiers. However, the Indians finally faced defeat. Signing the Treaty of Greenville in 1795, most of the chiefs agreed to move their people to the less settled northwestern part of the territory.

Many settlers arrived in the Northwest Territory by boat, traveling down the Ohio River or along the shores of the Great Lakes. Cincinnati, Ohio, was one

Indian tribes sign the Treaty of Greenville at Fort Greenville, Ohio.

of the first cities founded in the territory. The city thrived on river trade, selling goods such as salt pork and iron tools to settlers and pioneers moving farther west. The poet Henry Wadsworth Longfellow gave Cincinnati the nickname, "Queen of the West."

By 1803 Ohio had enough citizens to become a state. In time, other parts of the Northwest Territory became the states of Indiana, Illinois, Michigan, and Wisconsin. By then the Northwest Territory was no longer the frontier. It was full of farms and towns from which people left for land farther west.

Chapter Two

Trails Westward

As settlers were still arriving in the Northwest Territory, new frontiers arose in other parts of the continent. Explorers, traders, planters, and miners all found reasons to set out along the new trails.

The Voyage of Lewis and Clark

In 1803, the same year that Ohio settlers voted for statehood, the United States made a bargain for a huge new piece of land west of the Northwest Territory border. President Thomas Jefferson made this "Louisiana purchase" from France. Jefferson lost no time in sending official explorers to cross the new territory. They were to find out all they could about the land, its rivers, plants, animals, and Indians. And, they were to look for a good trade route all the way to the Pacific Ocean. Jefferson chose his secretary, Meriwether Lewis, to head the expedition. Lewis selected an old army friend and officer, William Clark, to help him.

Lewis and Clark and their forty-man Corps of Discovery set out westward in canoes along the Missouri River. The leaders kept journals on their trip, recording previously unknown animals such as the prairie dog, and telling about their meetings with Indian tribes. That winter, in a Mandan Indian village, they met a French trapper who offered his services as a guide. His fifteen-year-old Shoshone wife, Sacagawea, was from land far to the west and could also guide and translate. She turned out to be invaluable. Clark wrote, "The sight of this Indian woman convinced the Indians of our friendly intentions, as no woman ever accompanies a war party of Indians in this quarter."[2]

The Louisiana Purchase

British North America

Massachusetts
Vermont
New Hampshire
Oregon Country
New York
Rhode Island
Connecticut
New Jersey
Louisiana Purchase 1803
Indiana Territory
Ohio
Pennsylvania
Delaware
Maryland
Virginia
Kentucky
Tennessee
North Carolina
South Carolina
Mississippi Territory
Georgia
New Spain
Spanish Florida

Lewis and Clark reached the Pacific, and in the next year returned to the Mississippi in safety. They did not find an easy route for others to follow, but the whole nation celebrated their return. The voyage of Lewis and Clark strengthened Americans' interest in going farther west and discovering its possibilities.

Alabama Fever

Some of the Americans most interested in moving west were farmers in the southern states along the East Coast. The southern states favored slavery, because the farmers depended on slaves to grow cotton and other crops. When Congress outlawed slavery in the Northwest Territory the southern states acted. The states made sure it was not outlawed in the land to the west of them. In the South, the land was overused. At the same time, after 1792 it became possible to grow and sell much more cotton. The reason was Eli Whitney's invention of the cotton gin in that year. The cotton gin removed seeds from cotton, a slow and expensive job when done by hand. With the gin, it became profitable to raise enormous fields of cotton. The southerners headed toward the Alabama River area to find more land. Their urge to move west was called "Alabama fever."

The American newcomers did meet with some obstacles. One problem was that Spain still owned Florida, most of the Gulf Coast, and land from New Orleans westward. General Andrew Jackson of Tennessee voiced the feeling that most southerners shared—

Field workers tend a cotton crop in the South (below). Eli Whitney's cotton gin (left) removed the seeds from cotton, a valuable cash crop.

A painting depicts the forced march into modern-day Oklahoma along the Trail of Tears.

Spain should get out of North America. The War of 1812 between the United States and Britain gave Jackson a reason to enter New Orleans. He defeated British forces there, and a few years later his troops fought the Spanish in Florida. By 1819 Spain had given up its claims to all land east of the Mississippi.

Indians living on the land presented a second problem to the westward-moving southerners. Indian removal was a solution proposed by government leaders. Andrew Jackson, now president, signed a law in 1830 that required tribes east of the Mississippi to move from their homelands to new territory west of the river, in present-day Oklahoma. Some tribes left peacefully, but some resisted. The Cherokee tribe was forced westward, and gave the removal trail its famous name: the Trail of Tears.

Owners of new plantations across the South benefited from another invention as they laid out fields on rich riverside land: the steamboat. These boats allowed planters to bring their crops to market and helped make New Orleans a major world port. Few southerners questioned the way of life being established across the land in those years, or the fact that it depended on the institution of slavery.

The Oregon Trail

As settlers entered the southeastern part of the country, missionaries and fur trappers followed in the steps of Lewis and Clark farther west. A few missionaries established themselves early in Oregon's Willamette Valley, arriving there by ship. Trappers made their way into the Rocky Mountains, eager for a fresh bounty of beaver furs. In the 1820s and 1830s, fur companies arranged rendezvous, big yearly meetings, in the Rockies. Trappers and Indians arrived from all over the mountains to trade in their furs, drink, and celebrate. One of the trappers, Jedediah Smith, was the first non-Indian to find the great South Pass across the Rocky Mountains.

The South Pass proved to be an important link in forming a trail to Oregon country. The Oregon Trail reached from Independence, Missouri, all the way to the Pacific at the mouth of the Columbia River. Missionary Marcus Whitman led the first large wagon train across it in 1843.

A thousand people traveled with Whitman, and they set the pattern for other large migrations along the trail for years to come. Farming tools, a few clothes, and food for the trip were packed into "prairie schooners," covered wagons that looked like sailing ships on the prairie grass. The going was often hard. One man told of a rough spot: "Complete quagmire. Our animals give out fast. The River is lined with dead horses Mules & Oxen, shattered wagons in every direction."[3]

"Manifest Destiny"

Still, hope kept people going. The Mormons traveled mostly on foot along a variation of the Oregon Trail called the Overland Trail. They had been mistreated because of their religion and were seeking a new home. The Mormons founded Salt Lake City and helped create the state of Utah.

Both Britain and the United States had claimed the land where the Oregon Trail ended. As Americans poured in, the United States' goal of growing from coast to coast was becoming a reality. In 1845 a newspaper editor wrote that America's western expansion was meant to be: It was "**manifest destiny.**" A year later President Polk reached an agreement with Britain which gave all of the Oregon

Overland Routes to California

country to the United States. In time it became the states of Oregon and Washington.

The California Gold Rush

Just two years after the Oregon country became a U.S. territory, the land just south of it was rocked by a sudden discovery. A builder, James Marshall, saw shiny metal in a stream at a mill. He cried, "I believe I have found a gold mine!"[4] The summer of 1849 brought miners from all over North America and around the world. These "forty-niners" pumped up the population of California and helped bring the far West into the United States.

In the end, services to the miners made more people rich than the gold itself. When the gold rush began, California was part of a vast western part of North America very recently won by the United

After the gold rush of 1849 the population of California boomed. Growth was especially high in the port city of San Francisco.

States from Mexico. With the inrush of people, San Francisco became a metropolis, serving ships and selling supplies. Sacramento, the town nearest the gold fields, was made the capital of the new state of California which was accepted into the union in 1850.

After the California gold rush, prospectors were eager to find valuable minerals elsewhere in the West. Silver mines opened just across California's border in Nevada in 1859, and gold was struck in Colorado, Idaho, and Montana in the 1860s. People who rushed to the frontier to get rich quick often stayed to work or farm. They formed part of the growing population of the West.

Chapter  Three

The Spanish West

The California forty-niners came into a land which had recently been ruled by Spain. In the 1500s Spain conquered much of South and Central America. From their colonial capital at Mexico City they sent soldiers, priests, and colonists northward into the North American Southwest, and later into California. There they established ways of living that gave these parts of the West a special flavor. Mexico gained its independence from Spain in 1821. Only after that did the old Spanish West come into much contact, and conflict, with traders and settlers from the United States.

Spain's effort to colonize North America began when a Spanish army left Mexico City and marched up the Rio Grande in 1598. Spanish colonists settled in small villages, each with a **mission** and possibly a fort, surrounded by fields and ranches. Landowners, including the priests of the missions, introduced new plants to the region. They grew olives, grapes, citrus fruits, peaches, and wheat. They brought cattle, sheep, and horses to North America, too.

Spanish Ways in New Mexico and California

In 1609 Santa Fe was established as the capital of Spain's northernmost lands, called New Mexico. Ranchers there took Pueblo land for grazing or crops, and employed Indians as workers—sometimes by force. Many Indians grew angry when the missionaries tried to end Pueblo religious practices. One Pueblo holy man, named Pope, led a highly organized revolt in 1680. Pueblo warriors drove the Spanish out of New Mexico, and they did not return for twelve years. With time, however, Spanish villages took root.

The New Mexico pattern of settlement, based on missions and forts, was used again later in California. Governor Gaspar de Portola was sent in 1769 to establish Spanish rule along the coast. Working with him was Father Junípero Serra, a leader of Franciscan monks. In time the Franciscans established twenty-one missions from San Diego to Sonoma. Many of these missions and six presidios (forts) became the kernels of large California cities, including San Diego, San Francisco, and San Jose.

The missions combined the roles of church, farm, home, and town. The monks offered Indians the Christian faith, plus food and protection from enemies.

Father Junípero Serra (right) and other Spanish monks brought Christianity to the American Southwest. Mission San Diego de Alcalá (below), built in 1769, is one of California's many missions.

In return, Indians lived on the mission grounds and did all the work of building and farming that made the missions wealthy. However, many mission Indians grew sick and died of European diseases and malnutrition. Many were forced to work at missions and were treated like slaves or children.

Texas and the Mexican War

Across the Spanish West from California lay the area called Texas. Only a handful of Spanish villages were there in the early 1800s, when pioneers from the United States began to show an interest in this fertile land. One of them wrote, "it does not appear possible that there can be a land more lovely."[5] Stephen Austin, a pioneer from Connecticut, gained permission from the new nation of Mexico to lead three hundred American families to their own colony, under Mexican rule. Many pioneers from the United States followed them into Texas, both legally and illegally.

The increasing population of Americans in Texas began to alarm the Mexican government, especially when American Texans began to call for independence. Fighting began. In October 1836 the Mexican army killed every American defending an old mission called the Alamo in the city of San Antonio. News of the slaughter at the Alamo infuriated the Texans. In a battle at the San Jacinto River, they defeated the Mexicans. Mexican president Antonio de Santa Anna was forced to sign a paper allowing Texas to become an independent country.

Texans make their last stand at the Alamo. The Mexican
victory spurred American anger toward Mexico.

Claiming the Land

Texas asked to become part of the United States and was accepted into the Union in 1845. Mexico was horrified that the United States had taken Texas. Fighting along the border led to all-out war between Mexico and the United States.

President Polk used the war as an excuse to claim all of Mexico's northern territories, including New Mexico and California. An American army walked into New Mexico's capital, Santa Fe, and took it without a shot. When news of the Mexican war reached the West Coast, a handful of eager men declared California independent. This "republic" under a bear flag lasted only a month before American soldiers arrived to place California under the U.S. flag.

Marines were sent to Mexico City to force Santa Anna to sign a peace treaty granting New Mexico and California to the United States. The United States filled out its victory a few years later by buying a strip of borderland from Mexico, the Gadsden Purchase. In addition to Texas, the huge area gained through the war eventually became the states of California, Nevada, Utah, Arizona, and New Mexico, plus parts of Kansas and Colorado.

The Cowboy's Realm

All across the old Spanish West, from California to Texas, cattle were a very important source of wealth. In dry western lands cattle could find pasture where crops failed.

Several men raise a homemade bear flag to declare California's independence after hearing the news of Mexico's defeat.

The first cattle brought from Spain were allowed to run free on ranges, rounded up only once a year. Vaqueros, men on horseback, drove the cattle from place to place and tended them. Their tools and traditions included the lasso, chaps, silver decorations, the wide hat, the rodeo, and the branding iron. In

Cowboys round up a bull on the open range.

English, vaquero means cowboy. European Americans worked as cowboys, but as many as a third of the West's cowboys in the later 1800s were of Mexican, Indian, or African American descent.

Successful cattle ranching depended on open land without fences. Owners sorted out their animals by brand, and had some of them driven over long distances to market once a year. When railroads were built to the West in the 1860s, cattle could be driven shorter distances to railroad stations. However, the railroads also brought the beginning of the end of open range ranching. For riding on those same rails were thousands of new farmers who would build fences across the land.

Chapter Four

The Last Pioneers

By 1850 the United States had claimed land all the way from the Atlantic to the Pacific, between Canada and Mexico. Yet few settlers and traders moved into the center of the continent. Few pioneers were living on the vast Great Plains. In the second half of the century, railroads pushed their way across the plains, farmers took land, and towns grew up there. The growth had a price, though: the death or displacement of thousands of Native American people.

Homesteaders and Railroads

The Civil War lasted from 1861 to 1865, and afterward, many Americans from the North and South, including newly freed slaves, hoped for a fresh start in the West. The government passed a law during the war to encourage pioneers: the Homestead Act. This law allowed anyone to go westward to the Great Plains region and claim 160 acres of land. The homesteader only had to improve part of the land, build a house on it, and live there for five years. After that, the homesteader became the owner.

The government was not the only source of western land for settlers. Railroad companies were given land by the government if they would lay rails in the West. They then sold the land to settlers for profit, and to increase use of the railroads. In 1867 the first cattle were shipped by rail from the new **railhead** at Abilene, Kansas. Only two years later the Central Pacific and Union Pacific railroads met at Promontory Point,

A locomotive pushes through the American West.

A golden stake is driven in at Promontory Point, Utah, at a ceremony linking the Union and Central Pacific railways.

Utah. A golden spike marked the completion of the first transcontinental railroad.

The railroads made it easier for people to get to western land, and other inventions made it easier to farm there. John Deere's steel plow cut through the tough prairie **sod** much better than earlier plows had done. The mechanical reaper allowed people to harvest much more. And barbed wire, invented in 1873, permitted easy fencing to keep wild animals and cattle off large fields.

People from all over the United States and immigrants from all over the world poured into the Great Plains. They found vast grasslands with few trees, and they lived with the threat of prairie fire, grasshopper invasions, and **drought**. Some gave up and went back, but some families succeeded. Where there were not enough trees, settlers built houses from squares of grass-covered sod. Where water was scarce, they drew it up from deep wells using windmills. Pioneer women faced harder work than most women in the "civilized" East, but they also gained rights and freedoms sooner.

Indians and Expansion

Between 1870 and 1890 Kansas and Nebraska alone gained a million people each. But this boom in population meant terrible trouble for the Native Americans living on the plains. Many tribes had long made their homes there, most of them crisscrossing the plains on horseback in pursuit of their main game

Continually crowded by settlers, Indians sought to move farther west.

animal, the bison. They disliked the newcomers who were taking up land and killing game. Bison in particular were mowed down by pioneers, especially for the bison hide. Angry Indians sometimes attacked, and in response, the U.S. Army built new forts along the trails and sent companies of soldiers westward.

The government's main aim was to keep the Indians inside certain areas where they would not encounter settlers. In a series of treaties made with various chiefs, the government tried to pay off the Indians and convince them to stay in place. But the tribes were used to moving with the game. "If you tie a horse to a stake, do you expect he will grow fat?" asked Chief Joseph of the Nez Percé. "If you pen an Indian up on a small spot of earth, and compel him to stay there, he will not be contented."[6]

Chief Joseph was an active leader in the fight against Indian removal.

Even the **reservations** created by the government were continually eaten away. In Dakota Territory, for example, the Sioux and Cheyenne were granted rights to the Black Hills area. In 1873, though, gold was discovered there. The government tried to remove the Indians to a reservation elsewhere. Patrolling the Black Hills, General George Armstrong Custer and his soldiers attacked Sioux and Cheyenne men along the Little Bighorn River. The Indians killed Custer and his entire force. The Battle of the Little Bighorn frightened many Americans. The government decided to force all remaining free Indians onto definite reservations.

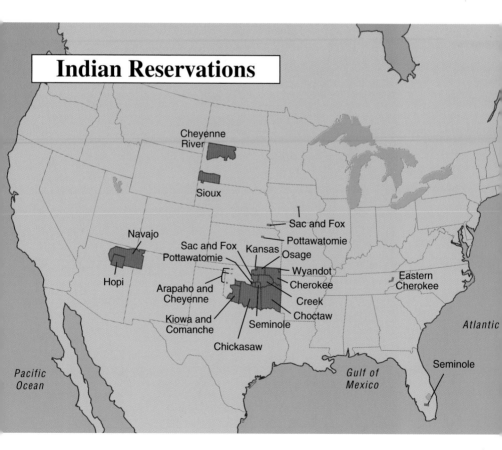

Indian Reservations

By the end of the 1800s opinions about the Indians had changed again. A new law, the Dawes Act, required that reservations be divided up among tribe members instead of being held by the whole group. However, swindlers got much of the land, and tribes lost strength with their acres. Oklahoma Territory included the land that had been granted to tribes from east of the Mississippi in the 1830s. Even this area was opened for homesteading beginning in 1889. People mobbed the border, then raced madly to claim former Indian land as the last homesteads of the frontier.

From the Yukon to Hawaii

As the 1800s ended and the West filled with people, Americans realized that many of the best aspects of western lands could easily be lost. In some places ruined earth and empty "ghost towns" showed where farming, lumbering, or mining had harmed the land. Where game had been plenty, animals were becoming extinct. Naturalist John Muir led a drive to save some of the West's most beautiful places as national parks. Yellowstone became the first of these in 1872. The U.S. Department of the Interior, created in 1849, took on more duties in regulating mining and lumbering.

Meanwhile the frontier was still moving. Back in 1857 Secretary of State William Seward bought Alaska from Russia. His deal was called "Seward's folly" because few people saw the use of all that frozen land. In the 1890s, however, gold was discovered along

Mount McKinley rises above Nugget Pond in Alaska, where gold was discovered in the 1890s.

the Yukon River in Canada, and then in Alaska. A last gold rush took people far to the north. And, in 1898, westward across the sea, the United States gained the island of Hawaii as a result of war with Spain.

The westward expansion of the United States was a complicated piece of history not all bad or all good.

For many people living today, the West is part of family history, as well as national history. There are as many views of the movement westward as there were people who experienced it.

It can be said that the frontier closed when Arizona became the last of the forty-eight adjoined states in 1912, or when Alaska and Hawaii were admitted to the Union in 1959. In a way, the frontier still exists as part of the American way of thinking. The spirit of the frontier may be any place where people look for a new home and a fresh start.

Notes

Chapter One: A Changing Frontier
1. Quoted in Edward S. Barnard, ed., *Story of the Great American West.* Pleasantville, NY: Reader's Digest, 1977, p. 21.

Chapter Two: Trails Westward
2. Quoted in Robert V. Hine and John Mack Faracher, *The American West: A New Interpretive History.* New Haven, CT: Yale University Press, 2000, p. 137.
3. Henry Wellencamp, quoted in Arthur King Peters, *Seven Trails West.* New York: Abbeville Press, 1996, p. 100.
4. Quoted in Hine and Faracher, *The American West,* p. 234.

Chapter Three: The Spanish West
5. Quoted in Barnard, ed. *Story of the Great American West,* p. 124.

Chapter Four: The Last Pioneers
6. Chief Joseph, *An American Indian's View of Indian Affairs.* Kirkwood, MO: The Printery, 1973, p. 43.

Glossary

drought: Period of very dry weather when crops cannot grow; common on the Great Plains.

manifest destiny: The idea that the United States was meant by God or fate to stretch its borders all the way to the Pacific.

mission: A church and group of people placed in a new or foreign land with the purpose of teaching and spreading religion and helping the native peoples.

railhead: Station at the farthest end of railroad tracks; cattle were driven to railheads when railroads first appeared in the Southwest.

reservations: Land set aside for Indian tribes to live on; often very undesirable land.

sod: Earth held together by grass roots; sod was cut into large bricks for house-building on the treeless plains.

station: Combination fort and village, a form of settlement common in Kentucky, Tennessee, and the Northwest Territory.

For Further Exploration

Judy Alter, *Pioneer Women of the Old West*. Minneapolis: Compass Point Books, 2001. This easy book tells about the roles of western women (including Indians, Spanish, and others) and the lives of particular women during the settlement period.

Paul Erickson, *Daily Life on a Southern Plantation, 1853*. New York: Lodestar Books, 1998. This large-format book details plantation life across the South in pictures and words; a time line at the end is helpful.

The West, dir. Stephen Ives, and prod. Ken Burns. Series of nine videocassettes. Santa Monica, CA: PBS Home Video, 1996. An excellent video series on the West, originally produced for public television, with emphasis on the settlement of the Great Plains and conflicts with the Indians there.

Bobbie Kalman, *Life in the Old West: Who Settled the West?* New York: Crabtree, 1999. Many old drawings, photos, and color paintings illustrate this overview of the many kinds of people who settled across America.

David C. King, *Wild West Days: Discover the Past with Fun Projects, Games, Activities and Recipes.* New York: John Wiley and Sons, 1998. Learn by doing with these authentic activities, sprinkled with stories from history.

Stuart Murray, *Wild West.* New York: DK Eyewitness Books, 2001. This book covers many topics associated with the West, each lavishly illustrated with wonderful pictures and photos of objects, many from the Smithsonian Institution.

Marc Tyler Nobleman, *The Battle of Little Bighorn.* Minneapolis: Compass Point Books, 2002. A short but thorough and beautifully illustrated account of the battle, its causes, and the aftermath.

Oregon Trail II. CD-ROM interactive game. Minneapolis: Minnesota Educational Computing, 1996. This highly popular CD-ROM makes the user a traveler on the Oregon Trail, making decisions and solving problems.

R. Conrad Stein, *How We Lived on the Old Western Frontier.* New York: Benchmark Books, 2000. An excellent history of ways of life in the Northwest Territory, Kentucky, and Tennessee, with good color illustrations and maps.

Index

Picture Credits

Cover photo: © Smithsonian American Art Museum/Art Resource

© Bettmann/CORBIS, 25

© The Corcoran Galley of Art/CORBIS, 15 (bottom)

© Corel Corporation, 28, 34, 38

© Philip James Corwin/CORBIS, 23 (bottom)

© Kevin Fleming/CORBIS, 15 (top)

© Robert Holmes/CORBIS, 23 (top)

© Hulton/Archive by Getty Images, 8, 31

Chris Jouan, 13, 19, 36

Library of Congress, 35

Ohio Historical Society, 11

Oklahoma Historical Society, 16

Private Collection/Bridgeman Art Library, 32

© Réunion des Musées Nationaux/Art Resource, 20

© Scala/Art Resource, 5, 9

© Smithsonian American Art Museum/Art Resource, 7

© Stock Montage, Inc., 27

About the Author

Cathryn J. Long writes nonfiction books for young people in areas of civics, history, and world affairs. She has recently written about the Cherokee and about ancient native Americans, and is taking part in a computer project for teaching about the earthwork and mound building cultures of the Ohio Valley.